Francis Frith's

VICTORIAN & EDWARDIAN
YORKSHIRE

PHOTOGRAPHIC MEMORIES

Francis Frith's

Victorian & Edwardian
YORKSHIRE

◆

Clive Hardy

British Library Cataloguing in Publication Data

Victorian & Edwardian Yorkshire
Clive Hardy
ISBN 1-85937-154-x

Frith Book Company Ltd
Frith's Barn, Teffont,
Salisbury, Wiltshire SP3 5QP
Tel: +44 (0) 1722 716 376
Email: info@frithbook.co.uk
www.frithbook.co.uk

Printed and bound in Great Britain

Front Cover: Bradford, Tyrrel Street 1903 **49713**

Contents

FRANCIS FRITH: *Victoria*

FRANCIS FRITH, Victorian founder of the world-famous photographic archive, was a complex and fascinating man. A devout Quaker and a highly successful Victorian businessman, he was both philosophic by nature and pioneering in outlook.

By 1855 Francis Frith had already established a wholesale grocery business in Liverpool, and sold it for the astonishing sum of £200,000, which is the equivalent today of over £15,000,000. Now a multi-millionaire, he was able to indulge his passion for travel. As a child he had pored over travel books written by early explorers, and his fancy and imagination had been stirred by family holidays to the sublime mountain regions of Wales and Scotland. 'What a land of spirit-stirring and enriching scenes and places!' he had written. He was to return to these scenes of grandeur in later years to 'recapture the thousands of vivid and tender memories', but with a different purpose. Now in his thirties, and captivated by the new science of photography pioneering journeys occupied him from 1856 until 1860.

INTRIGUE AND ADVENTURE

He took with him on his travels a specially-designed wicker carriage that acted as both dark-room and sleeping chamber. These far-flung journeys were packed with intrigue and adventure. In his life story, written when he was sixty-three, Frith tells of being held captive by bandits, and of fighting 'an awful midnight battle to the very point of surrender with a deadly pack of hungry, wild dogs'. Sporting flowing Arab costume, Frith arrived at Akaba by camel seventy years before Lawrence, where he encountered 'desert princes and rival sheikhs, blazing with jewel-hilted swords'.

During these extraordinary adventures he was assiduously exploring the desert regions bordering the Nile and patiently recording the antiquities and peoples with his camera. He was the first photographer to venture beyond the sixth cataract. Africa was still the mysterious 'Dark Continent', and Stanley and Livingstone's historic meeting was a decade into the future. The conditions for picture taking confound belief. He laboured for hours in his wicker dark-room in the sweltering heat of the desert, while the volatile chemicals fizzed dangerously in their trays. Often he was forced to work in remote tombs and caves where conditions

were cooler. Back in London he exhibited his photographs and was 'rapturously cheered' by members of the Royal Society. His reputation as a photographer was made overnight. An eminent modern historian has likened their impact on the population of the time to that on our own generation of the first photographs taken on the surface of the moon.

VENTURE OF A LIFE-TIME

Characteristically, Frith quickly spotted the opportunity to create a new business as a specialist publisher of photographs. He lived in an era of immense and sometimes violent change. For the poor in the early part of Victoria's reign work was a drudge and the hours long, and people had precious little free time to enjoy themselves.

Most had no transport other than a cart or gig at their disposal, and had not travelled far beyond the boundaries of their own town or village. However, by the 1870s, the railways had threaded their way across the country, and Bank Holidays and half-day Saturdays had been made obligatory by Act of Parliament. All of a sudden the ordinary working man and his family were able to enjoy days out and see a little more of the world.

With characteristic business acumen, Francis Frith foresaw that these new tourists would enjoy having souvenirs to commemorate their days out. In 1860 he married Mary Ann Rosling and set out with the intention of photographing every city, town and village in Britain. For the next thirty years he travelled the country by train and by pony and trap, producing fine photographs of seaside resorts and beauty spots that were keenly bought by millions of Victorians. These prints were painstakingly pasted into family albums and pored over during the dark nights of winter, rekindling precious memories of summer excursions.

THE RISE OF FRITH & CO

Frith's studio was soon supplying retail shops all over the country. To meet the demand he gathered about him a small team of photographers, and published the work of independent artist-photographers of the calibre of Roger Fenton and Francis Bedford. In order to gain some understanding of the scale of Frith's business one only has to look at the catalogue issued by Frith & Co in 1886: it

runs to some 670 pages, listing not only many thousands of views of the British Isles but also many photographs of most European countries, and China, Japan, the USA and Canada – note the sample page shown above from the hand-written *Frith & Co* ledgers detailing pictures taken. By 1890 Frith had created the greatest specialist photographic publishing company in the world, with over 2,000 outlets – more than the combined number that Boots and WH Smith have today! The picture on the right shows the *Frith & Co* display board at Ingleton in the Yorkshire Dales. Beautifully constructed with mahogany frame and gilt inserts, it could display up to a dozen local scenes.

POSTCARD BONANZA

◆

The ever-popular holiday postcard we know today took many years to develop. In 1870 the Post Office issued the first plain cards, with a pre-printed stamp on one face. In 1894 they allowed other publishers' cards to be sent through the mail with an attached adhesive halfpenny stamp. Demand grew rapidly, and in 1895 a new size of postcard was permitted called the court card, but there was little room for illustration. In 1899, a year after Frith's death, a new card measuring 5.5 x 3.5 inches became the standard format, but it was not until 1902 that the divided back came into being, with address and message on one face and a full-size illustration on the other. *Frith & Co* were in the vanguard of postcard development, and Frith's sons Eustace and Cyril continued their father's monumental task, expanding the number of views offered to the public and recording more and more places in Britain, as the coasts and countryside were opened up to mass travel.

Francis Frith died in 1898 at his villa in Cannes, his great project still growing. The archive he created continued in business for another seventy years. By 1970 it contained over a third of a million pictures of 7,000 cities, towns and villages. The massive photographic record Frith has left to us stands as a living monument to a special and very remarkable man.

Frith's Archive: *A Unique Legacy*

FRANCIS FRITH'S legacy to us today is of immense significance and value, for the magnificent archive of evocative photographs he created provides a unique record of change in 7,000 cities, towns and villages throughout Britain over a century and more. Frith and his fellow studio photographers revisited locations many times down the years to update their views, compiling for us an enthralling and colourful pageant of British life and character.

We tend to think of Frith's sepia views of Britain as nostalgic, for most of us use them to conjure up memories of places in our own lives with which we have family associations. It often makes us forget that to Francis Frith they were records of daily life as it was actually being lived in the cities, towns and villages of his day. The Victorian age was one of great and often bewildering change for ordinary people, and though the pictures evoke an impression of slower times, life was as busy and hectic as it is today.

We are fortunate that Frith was a photographer of the people, dedicated to recording the minutiae of everyday life. For it is this sheer wealth of visual data, the painstaking chronicle of changes in dress, transport, street layouts, buildings, housing, engineering and landscape that captivates us so much today. His remarkable images offer us a powerful link with the past and with the lives of our ancestors.

TODAY'S TECHNOLOGY

Computers have now made it possible for Frith's many thousands of images to be accessed almost instantly. In the Frith archive today, each photograph is carefully 'digitised' then stored on a CD Rom. Frith archivists can locate a single photograph amongst thousands within seconds. Views can be catalogued and sorted under a variety of categories of place and content to the immediate benefit of researchers. Inexpensive reference prints can be created for them at the touch of a mouse button, and a wide range of books and other printed materials assembled and published for a wider, more general readership - in the next twelve months over a hundred Frith local history titles will be published! The day-to-

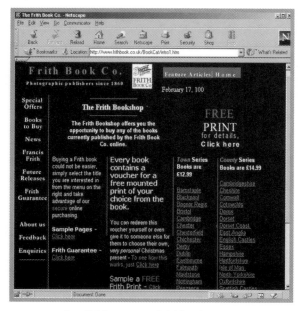

See Frith at www. frithbook.co.uk

day workings of the archive are very different from how they were in Francis Frith's time: imagine the herculean task of sorting through eleven tons of glass negatives as Frith had to do to locate a particular sequence of pictures! Yet the archive still prides itself on maintaining the same high standards of excellence laid down by Francis Frith, including the painstaking cataloguing and indexing of every view.

It is curious to reflect on how the internet now allows researchers in America and elsewhere greater instant access to the archive than Frith himself ever enjoyed. Many thousands of individual views can be called up on screen within seconds on one of the Frith internet sites, enabling people living continents away to revisit the streets of their ancestral home town, or view places in Britain where they have enjoyed holidays. Many overseas researchers welcome the chance to view special theme selections, such as transport, sports, costume and ancient monuments.

We are certain that Francis Frith would have heartily approved of these modern developments, for he himself was always working at the very limits of Victorian photographic technology.

THE VALUE OF THE ARCHIVE TODAY

Because of the benefits brought by the computer, Frith's images are increasingly studied by social historians, by researchers into genealogy and ancestory, by architects, town planners, and by teachers and schoolchildren involved in local history projects. In addition, the archive offers every one of us a unique opportunity to examine the places where we and our families have lived and worked down the years. Immensely successful in Frith's own era, the archive is now, a century and more on, entering a new phase of popularity.

THE PAST IN TUNE WITH THE FUTURE

Historians consider the Francis Frith Collection to be of prime national importance. It is the only archive of its kind remaining in private ownership and has been valued at a million pounds. However, this figure is now rapidly increasing as digital technology enables more and more people around the world to enjoy its benefits.

Francis Frith's archive is now housed in an historic timber barn in the beautiful village of Teffont in Wiltshire. Its founder would not recognize the archive office as it is today. In place of the many thousands of dusty boxes containing glass plate negatives and an all-pervading odour of photographic chemicals, there are now ranks of computer screens. He would be amazed to watch his images travelling round the world at unimaginable speeds through network and internet lines.

The archive's future is both bright and exciting. Francis Frith, with his unshakeable belief in making photographs available to the greatest number of people, would undoubtedly approve of what is being done today with his lifetime's work. His photographs, depicting our shared past, are now bringing pleasure and enlightenment to millions around the world a century and more after his death.

VICTORIAN & EDWARDIAN YORKSHIRE
An Introduction

Welcome to a selection from the Frith Collection of photographs of Yorkshire taken during the Victorian and Edwardian eras. The largest of all the English shires, Yorkshire once comprised an area of 3.75 million acres divided into three ridings; the West Riding was bigger than any other county, and the North Riding came in at a respectable fourth place. Just when the boundaries of Yorkshire were fixed is not known with any certainty, but its formation, along with Nottinghamshire, Leicestershire and Lincolnshire, occurred when the area was known as the Danelaw; we do know that the southern boundary of Yorkshire conformed pretty much to the old border between Northumbria and Mercia.

At the beginning of the 19th century, England was still a rural country: less than a third of the population lived in towns, and only one in five of those in a town of more than 20,000 inhabitants. In 1811 the total population for Yorkshire was given as 973,113. By the census of 1821 it had risen to 1,173,187. Of these, 799,357 lived in the West

Riding, with 190,449 in the East, and 183,381 in the North. The prospect of work attracted thousands of migrants from rural areas, but factory work in the early 19th century would have been unlike anything they had ever known before. There were strict hours of attendance, and the work was done at a pace set by the employer in virtually unregulated conditions. Factory workers, including children, worked long hours: Bradford mill owners were among those who imported orphans sent from London workhouses and used them as little better than slave labour. Children as young as five worked up to thirteen hours a day and were beaten to keep them awake. Living conditions were often appalling. Families were crowded into single rooms or cellars; sanitation usually consisted of a cess-pit, the contents of which invariably managed to contaminate the local water supply, a communal well. It took a number of outbreaks of cholera and thousands of deaths to galvanise the country into public health measures. However, it was not all work and no play. Men like Richard Oastler and John Wood petitioned parliament to improve working conditions in factories, to cut hours and to end child labour in the mills. By the 1850s some workers were getting a few days' holiday, even if it was without pay, and there was at least some time off at weekends. By the end of Victoria's reign, in Yorkshire as a whole only one in five people were still living in the country.

Some of the rises in population had been dramatic. The best-known is that of Middlesbrough, which in 1801 had consisted of just four houses, twenty-five people, a couple of cows and a few scraggy chickens. Things changed when the Stockton & Darlington Railway Co decided upon Middlesbrough as the location for staithes for the transfer of coals to ships. Joseph Pease was responsible not only for extending the railway, but also for laying out the new town; it consisted of a dozen or so streets of houses, a market square, a town hall, and a parish church. By 1841 the population had rocketed to 5463 inhabitants; the staithes were moving around 1.5 million tonnes of coal a year, and additional industries had been attracted to the area. That same year Henry Bolckow and John Vaughan opened an ironworks, and by 1873 Teesside was producing about one-third of the entire British output of iron.

With the rise of Middlesbrough came the North Riding's involvement in shipbuilding on a grand scale. Further down the coast at Whitby, a yard had been established by Thomas Turnbull & Son in 1840; they built wooden sailing ships before turning their attentions to building steam tramps. The problem with Whitby is that Turnbulls were restricted in the type of vessels they could build, for Whitby bridge imposed restrictions upon beam and dead weight tonnage. Ironmaking along the Tees, readily available supplies of coal and coke, a massive influx of people wanting work, and shipowners needing steamships, came together to produce an industry that rivalled those on the Wear and the Tyne. Rake, Kimber & Co opened a shipyard on the Tees in 1858 on a site now occupied by the transporter bridge. The 'De Brus' was the first iron ship to be built at Middlesbrough, but after completing only three more vessels the yard closed owing to lack of orders. It was taken over by Richardson, Duck & Co, who already had a yard at Stockton; it was they who put a young man by the name of Raylton Dixon in charge. By 1873 Raylton had secured the yard for himself and renamed it Raylton Dixon & Co. His first ship was the 2099 dead weight tonnes iron steamer 'Torrington' for the Commercial Steam Shipping Co. The yard went on to build ships for some of the great shipping companies of the late 19th and early 20th centuries, including Lamport & Holt, Elder Dempster, Hansa Line of Hamburg, Bergen Line, Wilson Line of Hull, and Houlder Line. Other shipyards on the Yorkshire side of the Tees were Smith's Dock at South Bank, and Robert Craggs & Co, which opened on land adjacent to Sir Raylton Dixon's yard.

There are far too many towns in the West Riding to be mentioned here - this is not a detailed economic and social history of the period - but some of the more influential were Sheffield, Leeds and Bradford. By 1870 Sheffield's population was approaching the 240,000 mark. In 1875 the town centre was redeveloped with the construction of Pinstone Street, Leopold Street and Surrey Street, and in 1893 the Council began a slum clearance programme in the Crofts, an area extending from the rear of the parish church to West Bar. Plans were drawn up for the erection of a new Town Hall befitting the newest city in the kingdom. It was finished in 1896, complete with a 210 ft high tower topped off with a bronze statue of Vulcan. However, it was not until 1898 that the city accountant broke the news to the ratepayers that the building had cost £182,000.

By the 17th century, Leeds was noted for woollen manufacture, dyeing, cropping and dressing. The twice-weekly Leeds cloth fair was considered the most important in Yorkshire; thousands of pounds-worth of cloth was traded every week. Diversification came during the 19th century: the ever-growing town attracted engineering firms, chemical and oil plants, tanneries and leatherworks, paper mills, print works and glassmaking factories. Firms like Fairbairn & Lawson manufactured flax and tow machinery; Kitson's Airedale Foundry turned out traction, stationary and ploughing engines under sub-contract for John Fowler; the Leeds Forge Co and Kirkstall Forge Co produced all types of castings. Leeds became a major centre for the manufacture of railway locomotives; some early players in the game were Todd, Kitson & Laird, Fenton, Murray & Jackson, and E B Wilson & Co. In 1861 the population of Leeds had passed the 200,000 mark; by 1881 it was over 300,000, and by 1901 it was over 425,000.

As with the majority of industrial towns, Leeds in the 1870s was smoke-begrimed and overcrowded, with 75 per cent of its inhabitants crammed into just 12.5 per cent of the total area of the borough. Housing conditions for many were appalling, to say the least. The influxes of migrants in search of work had resulted in cheap unregulated housing being thrown up, such as Johnson's Square, which consisted of fifteen single-room houses situated below the level of Charles Street. Camp Field off Water Lane comprised ninety-two back-to-back houses built in an area of 8750 square yards. With little thought being given to sewage disposal or water supply, infectious diseases were rife in working-class areas; in 1832 an outbreak of cholera killed 700; a further outbreak in 1848-49 killed 2000. A noted tourist attraction in Wellington Yard in 1872 was a midden covering 756 cubic feet; God help anyone who fell in it.

Though Leeds continued to play a major role in the woollen industry, competition was increasing, and a number of large mills were diversifying into doing their own dyeing and finishing. In 1891 woollen and clothing manufacturers were employing over 52,000 workers between them, but the growth over the previous ten years had been in engineering, other manufacturing, transport, professional and service sector areas, where a total of 55,000 jobs had been created.

Victorian and Edwardian Bradford was the centre of the woollen and worsted industry not only in this country, but throughout the world. Trading days at the Wool Exchange could be truly international, with buyers and sellers from many countries. It was said that no matter the type of wool or hair, a buyer would be found at the Bradford Exchange. Eager to maintain its position, especially as there was growing competition from the

French, Bradford opened a Technical School. Here innovation and ideas were encouraged; Bradford manufacturers strove to be at the forefront in both the design and quality of their goods. Even so, the late-Victorian traveller would have found Bradford a veritable forest of smoking mill chimneys interspersed with the often squalid housing of the workers. As with Leeds, Sheffield and a hundred other towns, the streams and brooks ran black with pollution and raw sewage. There were other industries. Bradford was on the western edge of the great Yorkshire coalfield, and because the coal was near to the surface, it could be mined relatively inexpensively. Also close by were the ironworks of Bowling and Low Moor. The city had already long had a cosmopolitan air

about it. Since the 1830s the wool trade had made Bradford an attractive proposition for people from Saxony, Prussia, Ireland, Italy, Austria-Hungary and Tsarist Russia. Redevelopment of the town centre began in the 1880s, when the Roadstones area was cleared to make way for Forster Square. Part of the redevelopment included a post office, which though impressive in its own right obscured the ascent to the Parish Church.

Titus Salt was one of the most influential people in the history of Bradford. The story of how Titus made his fortune is well known. His love affair with alpaca began when he spotted some unwanted bales in the warehouse. Taking a sample, he asked his father's opinion. His father advised him to leave well alone. Like most sons, Titus ignored his

Bradford, Manningham Lane 1902 48570

father, bought the entire shipment and had it woven. Alpaca soon caught on, and the rest, as they say, is history. What sets Titus apart from many other Bradford mill owners was his concern for his workers. Titus realised that a contented workforce meant better productivity, and that better productivity meant greater profits. Between 1850 and 1853 Titus built a new mill and township for his workers at Saltaire, a few miles outside Bradford. Complete with school, cottage hospital, almshouses and chapel, Saltaire gave Titus's employees a standard of accommodation far higher than most of them would ever have had in Bradford. However,

there was no pub - Titus was teetotal, and would have nothing to do with strong drink.

Doncaster, like Derby, had been transformed by the coming of the railways. It changed from an agricultural to an industrial town when it was chosen by the Great Northern Railway as the location for its locomotive and carriage and wagon workshops. Coal mining would also be a major employer, with the nearby pits of Brodsworth, Askern Main and Hatfield Main. The early years of the 20th century saw a boom in the opening of new collieries in South Yorkshire. In 1900 the Sheepbridge Coal & Iron Co acquired an interest in the

Doncaster, St Sepulchre Gate 1903 49850

Dinnington Main Coal Co; this enabled it to exploit the coalfield to the north of Kiveton Park. Near Doncaster, the first sod was cut at Brodsworth in 1905 and at Hatfield Main on 11 October 1911. The Maltby Main Colliery Co was formed in 1906 with capital of £350,000, and in 1912 John Brown & Co and Sheepbridge joined forces to create the Rossington Main Colliery Co to sink a new pit at Rossington. At Hatfield it took five years to reach Barnsley bed coal, struck at a depth of 852 yds. Rossington completed sinking in May 1915, and was equipped with plant capable of raising over 5000 tonnes a day.

But it was not all industry in Victorian and Edwardian Yorkshire. The East Riding, with its fertile arable land, supported thousands of farms. Although its industry was light when compared with the other Ridings, the city of Hull rose to become the third largest port in England and one of the major centres of the UK fishing industry. The West Riding included the watering places of Harrogate, Ilkley and Boston Spa. Harrogate was developed as a spa in the 1840s by the Duchy of Lancaster, the first public baths opening in 1842. By 1906 it was being described as having a 'high and bracing situation among the Yorkshire moors, and ranks with Bath and Buxton among the three chief inland watering-places of England. It consists of two parts, High and Low Harrogate, the former to the left of the station, the latter to the right. It is perhaps the most aristocratic of all the great English spas'. The sulphur springs, of which there were two strong and seventeen mild, were said to be efficacious 'for most affectations of the liver, jaundice, gout, rheumatism, and diseases of the skin. The six chalybeate springs are tonic and stimulant.

The so-called bog-springs, of which there are 34 in number, rise in a small piece of boggy ground a little to the West of the sulphur-springs, and though close together no two are exactly alike'.

Scarborough in the East Riding had first been developed as a spa town. Its waters were first discovered by a certain Mrs Farrow in c1626; the earliest building over the spa was little more than a wooden shelter built for the convenience of people wishing to drink the waters. Disaster struck in 1737 when a landslip destroyed the spa, and it was two years before it was able to be reopened. By this time the spa was housed in a pump-room, but this too was destroyed and replaced in 1839. Scarborough was now a major tourist attraction for the genteeler classes; this was reflected in the new spa buildings, which by the late 1850s included a concert hall. Scarborough continued to maintain its genteel airs and graces, and objected to the coming of the railway on the grounds that it wanted nothing to do with the great unwashed: 'the watering place has no wish for a greater influx of vagrants and those who have no money to spend'. Be that as it may, Scarborough did become popular with working people, though for a number of years it managed to maintain two distinct seasons: a fashionable one and a popular one.

This book is not a detailed history of Victorian and Edwardian Yorkshire; the introduction merely serves to set the scene and to give a flavour, if you like, of the time and the people. The pictures are accompanied by captions, which I hope you will find interesting and on occasion entertaining.

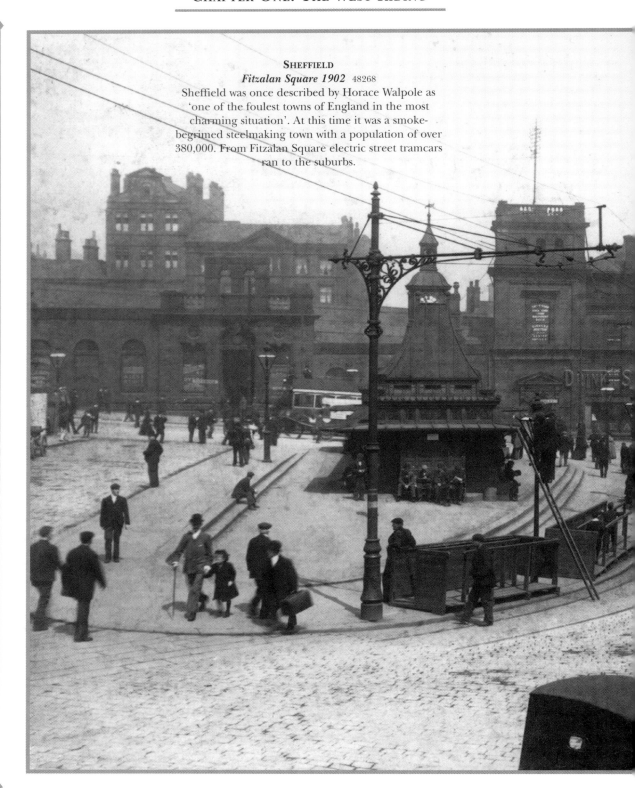

SHEFFIELD
Fitzalan Square 1902 48268
Sheffield was once described by Horace Walpole as
'one of the foulest towns of England in the most
charming situation'. At this time it was a smoke-
begrimed steelmaking town with a population of over
380,000. From Fitzalan Square electric street tramcars
ran to the suburbs.

SHEFFIELD, HIGH STREET 1900 45485

The High Street, sandwiched between Fargate and the junction of Chapel Street and the Market Place, was one of Sheffield's principal shopping streets. Here cabs await their next fares; prices and conditions were set by the local authority. Cabs could be hired by distance or by time - the latter depended upon how many passengers there were. Shoppers were not charged extra for 'ordinary' luggage.

SHEFFIELD, THE CRIMEAN MONUMENT 1893 31962

This is the junction of South Street and Union Street. The monument was erected to commemorate the Crimean War; as with many such monuments, it came complete with captured Russian cannon. Of more benefit to the locals were the new public lavatories built alongside.

SHEFFIELD, ST PAUL'S CHURCH 1893 31967
Construction of St Paul's began in 1720, but owing to a squabble over the right of presentation it was not opened until 1740. The dome was added in 1769.

ECCLESFIELD 1902 48937
Situated five miles north of Sheffield, Ecclesfield was industrialised by the late 18th century and was large enough to have its own workhouse. By 1821 the population had topped 7000; many were employed in nail making, file manufacturing, flax dressing and linen manufacturing.

ECCLESFIELD, THE POST OFFICE 1902 48938

The inn is getting a delivery, and the local post office seems to be a department store in miniature: it is a drapers and boot and shoe makers, and licensed to sell tobacco, cigars and patent medicines. The inn appears to have entered the tourist trade offering good accommodation for cyclists.

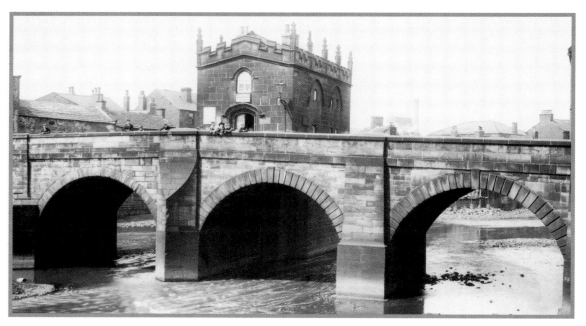

ROTHERHAM, BRIDGE CHAPEL 1895 36241

The Chapel of Our Lady standing on Rotherham Bridge dates from the 1480s; a similar structure at Wakefield was founded by Edward III in 1460. Rotherham Bridge was widened in 1805, but was restored to its original width in 1924. Wakefield Bridge was restored in the mid 19th century.

ROTHERHAM, CLIFTON PARK 1895 36244
Clifton House was designed by John Carr of York for the Rotherham ironmaster Joshua Walker, and completed in 1782. At this date Carr was one of the North's leading architects, having designed the Crescent at Buxton for the Duke of Devonshire. Clifton House is now a museum, and its parkland open to the public.

DONCASTER, ST GEORGE'S CHURCH 1893 31980
St George's parish church dates from the 1850s, and is considered to be one of Sir Gilbert Scott's finest designs. The distinctive tower stands 170 ft high, and the building is 170 ft long. It replaced the medieval church destroyed by fire in 1853.

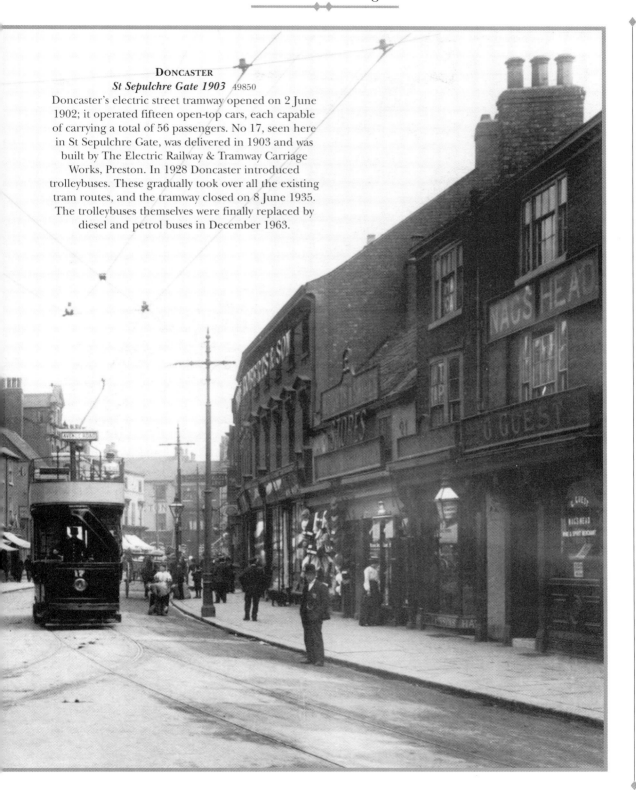

DONCASTER
St Sepulchre Gate 1903 49850

Doncaster's electric street tramway opened on 2 June 1902; it operated fifteen open-top cars, each capable of carrying a total of 56 passengers. No 17, seen here in St Sepulchre Gate, was delivered in 1903 and was built by The Electric Railway & Tramway Carriage Works, Preston. In 1928 Doncaster introduced trolleybuses. These gradually took over all the existing tram routes, and the tramway closed on 8 June 1935. The trolleybuses themselves were finally replaced by diesel and petrol buses in December 1963.

DONCASTER, THE YORK CITY & COUNTY BANK 1900 45112
One of Doncaster's finest takes an interest in the man from Frith. The York City & County Bank shares a part of its imposing building with a branch of the Home & Colonial, one of the most successful of all Victorian high street chains.

LEEDS, THE PARISH CHURCH 1891 28281
Dedicated to St John the Evangelist, the parish church was consecrated in 1634. The church was heavily restored during the 19th century, when its superb box pews were cut down and irreparably damaged. However, the two-deck pulpit and tester survived unscathed.

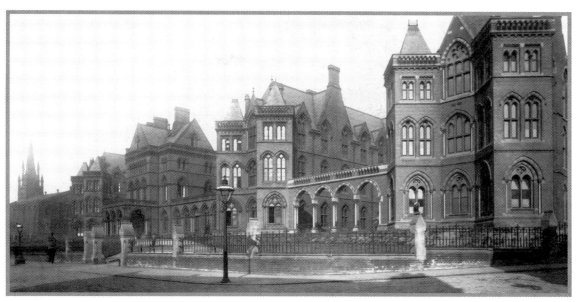

LEEDS, THE INFIRMARY 1894 34769

In 1809 the body of Mary Bateman was taken to an earlier infirmary in Leeds after her execution at York Castle. Over 2500 people paid 3d each to see her corpse, which was later handed over to the surgeons for dissection. Following a rather quaint Yorkshire custom, her skin was then tanned, cut into small pieces, and given out as souvenirs to anyone who applied.

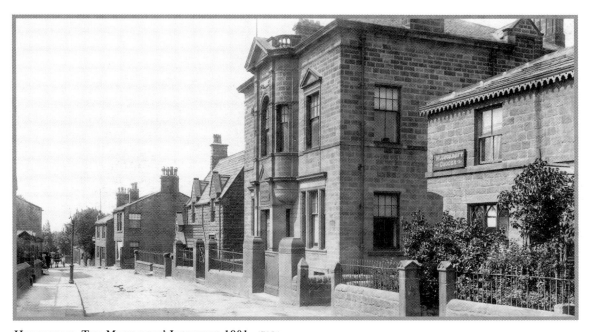

HORSFORTH, THE MECHANICS' INSTITUTE 1901 47134

Founded by George Birkbeck of Settle, the Mechanics' Institute movement spread rapidly during the mid 19th century. These places provided workers with opportunities to study a wide range of subjects, and offered the brightest the chance of gaining a place at university.

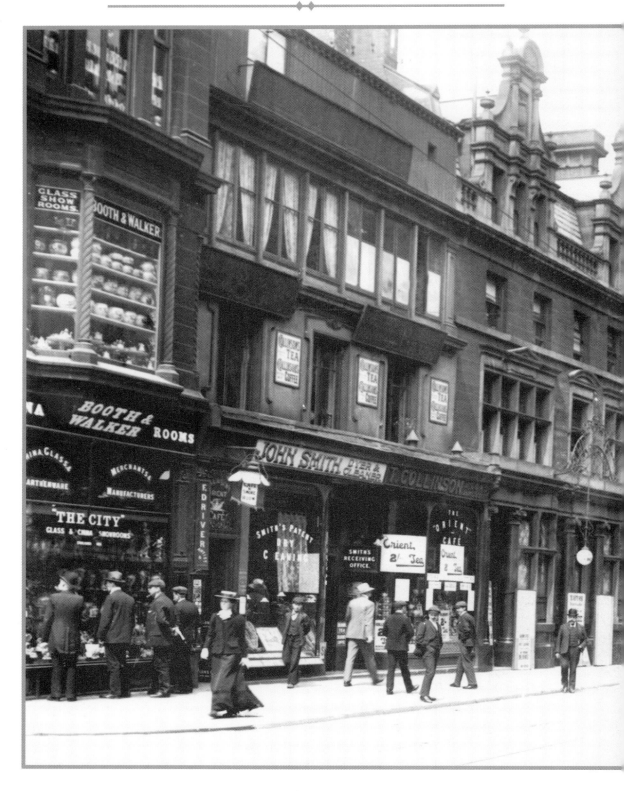

BRADFORD
Tyrrel Street 1903 49713
Bradford was the centre of the woollen and worsted
industry, even though trade with the United States
during the 1890s had been badly affected by the
McKinley Tariffs. The Bradford Exchange was truly
international, with manufacturers, agents and dealers
from around the world buying and selling wool or hair
of every imaginable type and quality.

BRADFORD, THE TOWN HALL 1897 39511

The Town Hall was completed in 1871 at a cost of £100,000. In April 1891 a searchlight was mounted on the tower as part of the authority's attempts to restore order following two days of civil unrest caused by strikers from Lister's Mill. Troops were called in to assist the police, and a number of baton charges and arrests were made before the strikers were finally broken.

BRADFORD, FORSTER SQUARE 1897 39506

A steam tram rattles through the square, whilst the plinth of Richard Oastler's statue affords a convenient place to stop and sit awhile. Oastler played a major role in ending child labour in the mills. Bradford mill owners worked children for up to thirteen hours a day, and often subjected them to beatings to keep them awake.

BRADFORD, MANNINGHAM LANE 1902 48570
The Theatre Royal is on the left, next door to the Royal Standard Hotel. This is where the greatest Victorian actor of them all, Sir Henry Irving, gave his last performance. After appearing here on 13 October 1905, Sir Henry retired to his hotel for the night, where he was taken ill and died.

SALTAIRE, THE STATION 1909 61871
Saltaire station lies on the Midland Railway route between Bradford and Skipton. Salt's Mill stands next to the line. When built it was the largest mill in Europe: it was six storeys high, its weaving shed held 1200 looms, and there was a workforce of over 3000.

BINGLEY, THE BOAT STATION 1894 34749
Boating on the Aire has been popular for decades, even if the waters were polluted with waste discharged from local mills. In the 19th century, the town was a centre for worsted weaving and textiles; a mill chimney-stack can be seen in the background.

BINGLEY, IN THE PARK 1894 34757
A drinking fountain complete with tin cups awaits those who need to quench their thirsts, possibly after walking from St David's Ruin by way of Beckfoot Lane. The ruin is in fact a folly built by Benjamin Ferdinand in 1796. It is supposed to resemble a ruined castle, and is similar to the folly at Mow Cop in Staffordshire.

HALIFAX, THE ROCKS 1893 33212

In the distance is Wainhouse Tower, 253 ft high, with over 400 steps and weighing in at about 9000 tonnes. It was built between 1871 and 1875 as a chimney to take away smoke from John Wainhouse's Washer Lane Dyeworks, but it was never used. In 1893 there was a plan to demolish it, but this was never carried out. In 1912 there was even a proposal to convert it into a crematorium.

HALIFAX, SOUTHGATE 1893 33206A

There is a fine display of rabbits, hares and chickens outside Yates & Sons, whilst in the next shop doorway along Mr Smith the fish-merchant takes a breather between serving customers. Across the road, the large gilt spectacles above a shop doorway tells customers that they have found Holdsworth the opticians.

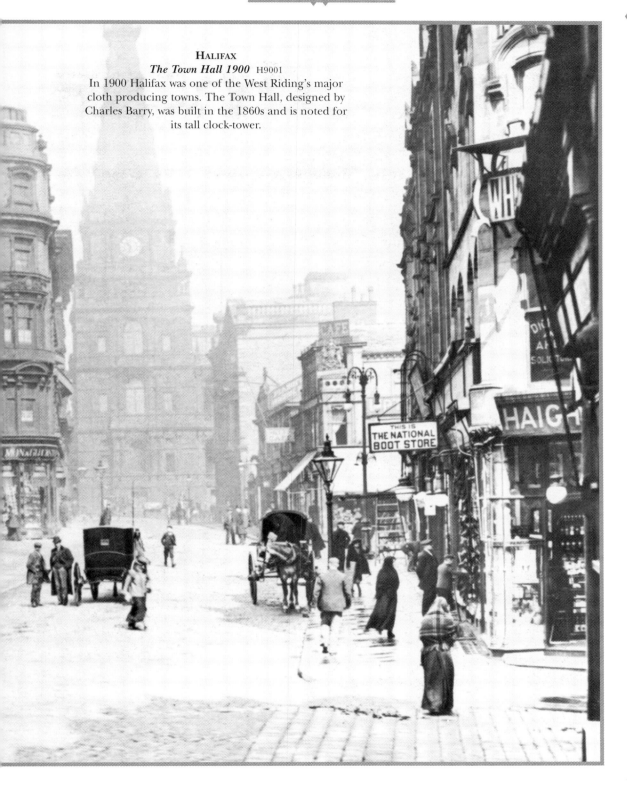

HALIFAX
The Town Hall 1900 H9001
In 1900 Halifax was one of the West Riding's major
cloth producing towns. The Town Hall, designed by
Charles Barry, was built in the 1860s and is noted for
its tall clock-tower.

SELBY, THE ABBEY CHURCH 1903 49863

SELBY
The Abbey Church 1903

Work began on the abbey church in c1100; the Benedictine monastery it once served had been founded by Benedict of Auxerre in 1069. Though the church was completed by about 1230, the chancel was rebuilt before 1300, and the nave clerestory by 1335. It survived the Dissolution to become the parish church for the town.

◆

SELBY
Gowthorpe Street 1901

In 1901 Selby was described as a small agricultural town with 7786 inhabitants; it was the traditional birthplace of Henry I, the only son of William the Conqueror to be born in England. Accommodation at the George was inexpensive: rooms were 2s, and dinner 2s. The Londesborough Arms, near the abbey church, offered lunch at 2s 6d a head.

SELBY, GOWTHORPE STREET 1901 47168

SELBY, THE BRIDGE 1901 48027
The timbered toll-bridge carrying the York road over the Ouse was erected in 1791, and was one of the earliest of its type in the country. It survived until replaced by a modern bridge in 1970.

BOSTON SPA, THE SPA BATHS 1897 39440
Situated on the lower Wharfe four miles southeast of Wetherby, Boston became a spa in the 18th century when a man named John Shires discovered a saline spring. For a few years Boston was a fashionable place, a place to see and be seen at.

BOSTON SPA, HOLY LANE 1893 32005
A sylvan setting down Holy Lane, Boston Spa.

Boston Spa, The Royal Hotel 1897 39434

Wealthy travellers on the Great North Road would make a detour to Boston to sample the pump room; many would put up at the Royal Hotel, a coaching inn. During the season there was a daily scheduled stagecoach service to Leeds and back. However, Boston could never hope to compete with Harrogate, and it eventually faded into obscurity.

Wetherby, North Street 1909 61731

Once an important coaching town on the Great North Road, Wetherby went into decline for a number of years as long-distance stagecoach travel lost out to the railways. By 1909, however, Wetherby was fighting back, attracting passing tourist trade, and gearing up for the automobile. The town boasted two AA-listed hotels with garaging for cars, and William Ward & Sons were the local AA agents.

WETHERBY, THE RIVER WHARFE AND THE BRIDGE 1909 61734

Wetherby was described in at least one guide as 'a town of no interest'. We see here the bridge built to carry the Great North Road over the Wharfe; behind it is a weir and an old mill. The bridge once echoed to the constant clatter of horse-drawn vehicles, but things had become a lot quieter with the coming of the railways.

KNARESBOROUGH, THE CASTLE C1873 6662

The first castle on the site is thought to have been built by Serlo de Burg, who received lands in the area from William the Conqueror. The fortress was extensively rebuilt during the early decades of the 14th century; the work was probably started by Piers Gaveston after being granted the lordship by Edward II.

KNARESBOROUGH, THE RAILWAY VIADUCT 1892 30604

This distinctive railway viaduct was the second to span the Nidd, the first having collapsed shortly after completion. In the background is St John's Church, which dates from the 13th and 14th centuries. In 1318 Scots raiders sacked the town, destroying between 140 and 160 properties. They attempted to fire St John's, but failed; for centuries afterwards the tower bore traces of burning.

KNARESBOROUGH, ST ROBERT'S CAVE 1892 30616

The cave is named after Robert Flower, a hermit, and son of a mayor of York, who lived here from about 1180 until his death in 1218, when he was buried in a tomb in the cave. The carved figure is thought to be 16th-century. The cave has a more infamous past, in that it was here that Eugene Aram hid the body of Daniel Clarke after he had murdered him.

HARROGATE

Parliament Street 1902 48977

On the left can be seen the huge gilt sign fronting Boots the Chemists, proclaiming that they are the 'largest chemists in the world'. Across the street is Tyler's shoe shop, and next to that H Waterlands grocery. Within a few years, Waterlands will have given way to a branch of Taylors Drug Stores, who will take on Boots and outdo them with an even larger gilt sign.

HARROGATE, STATION SQUARE 1902 48978
Here we see Station Square, with the 45-bed Station Hotel owned by the North Eastern Railway over on the left. In the background is the large and imposing store of Edward Standing Ltd; the Oriental Cafe; and the Central Hotel. The statue was raised in honour of Queen Victoria's jubilee in 1887.

HARROGATE, THE ROYAL PUMP ROOM 1902 48975
The Royal Pump Room opened at 7.00am dispensing sulphur and chalybeate water, which in 1902 cost 3d a glass. The roads leading to the Pump Room were often chained off to allow drinkers the opportunity of enjoying a leisurely constitutional to either the Crescent or Valley Gardens.

HARROGATE
The Royal Baths 1902

The Royal Baths cost nearly £100,000 to build; when they were opened in 1897, it was said that they were unequalled in decoration and roominess. The money lavished on providing Harrogate with the very best of facilities ensured that the town remained the most fashionable spa in the country for nearly fifty years.

◆

HARROGATE
The Prospect Hotel 1897

Most of the large hotels looked out over the Stray, 200 acres of land opened to the public in 1778. Rates at the Prospect were rooms from 4s 6d, dinner 6s. The Royal was slightly cheaper, with rooms from 4s, but the Royal Spa was more expensive with rooms there costing from 5s 6d.

HARROGATE, THE ROYAL BATHS 1902 48981

HARROGATE, THE PROSPECT HOTEL 1897 39423

HARROGATE
Crescent Gardens 1907 58648
For decades, music was a feature of everyday life during the season. Late morning concerts were held both at the Crescent and the Winter Gardens. In 1896 a Municipal Orchestra was formed under the leadership of J Sydney Jones; it survived until it was disbanded as an economy measure in 1930.

HARROGATE, THE CROWN HOTEL 1902 48972
In 1821, the Crown was the most expensive hotel in Lower Harrogate at 8s 6d a day including meals. By the time of our picture, rates were similar to those at the Prospect and the White Hart.

HARROGATE, THE GEORGE HOTEL 1902 48982
The 100-bed George Hotel was in a similar price range as the Wellington and the Adelphi. During the season, hotels charged the same daily rate (room, meals, service etc) even if guests took their meals elsewhere. At fashionable hotels such as the Prince of Wales and the Majestic, guests were expected to dress for dinner.

HARROGATE, THE WELLINGTON HOTEL 1902 48984
Not all visitors to Harrogate came for the waters and the social season; many used it as a base for excursions. The Wellington offered guests room, meals and service at an all-in daily rate of between 10s and 12s.

RIPLEY, THE CROSS & STAR HOTEL 1893 32018
Four miles north of Harrogate, Ripley in 1893 consisted of little more than one broad street and was the property of the Ingilby family of Ripley Castle. In the 1820s the slightly dotty Sir William Amcotts Ingilby had many of the old cottages replaced by Tudor-style or Gothic houses in an attempt to remodel the village along Alsatian lines. He even renamed the village hall the Hotel de Ville.

RIPLEY, THE CASTLE c1861 7362

The tower to the right of the picture belongs to All Saints, a 15th-century church with 16th-century additions, which suffered from a 19th-century restoration. On the left is Ripley Castle, seat of the Ingilby family for over 700 years. An earlier castle on the site was replaced during the 16th century, though the gatehouse could be 15th-century. In the 1780s the Ingilbys spent a small fortune in commissioning extensive rebuilding.

ILKLEY, SPENCER GARDENS 1906 56477

Ilkley remained an obscure place until 1850, when the local spring waters were declared beneficial to health, if taken in conjunction with a dietary regime, brisk walks on the moors, and constitutionals around the town and its parks.

ILKLEY
Semon's Convalescent Home 1900
Ilkley became yet another spa town: hotels, villas, convalescent homes and hydropathic establishments sprang up as investment poured in. A week's treatment at either the Craig Lands or the Ilkley Wells Hydro cost between 2 and 3 guineas; rates for rooms at the top-of-the-range Middleton Hotel started from 5s a day, while at the other end of the scale the Lister's Arms was described as 'unpretending'.

❖

SKIPTON
The Castle Courtyard 1893
Held by the de Clifford family for 375 years, Skipton is best known for its role during the English Civil War, when Sir John Mallory and his 300-strong garrison withstood a Parliamentarian siege that lasted for three years. When the garrison finally surrendered, its stand was recognised by the Parliamentarians, who allowed it to march out with full honours of war, fully armed with drums beating and colours flying. One of the features of the courtyard is the yew tree, which is still standing and is thought to be more than 300 years old.

ILKLEY, SEMON'S CONVALESCENT HOME 1900 45152

SKIPTON, THE CASTLE COURTYARD 1893 33162

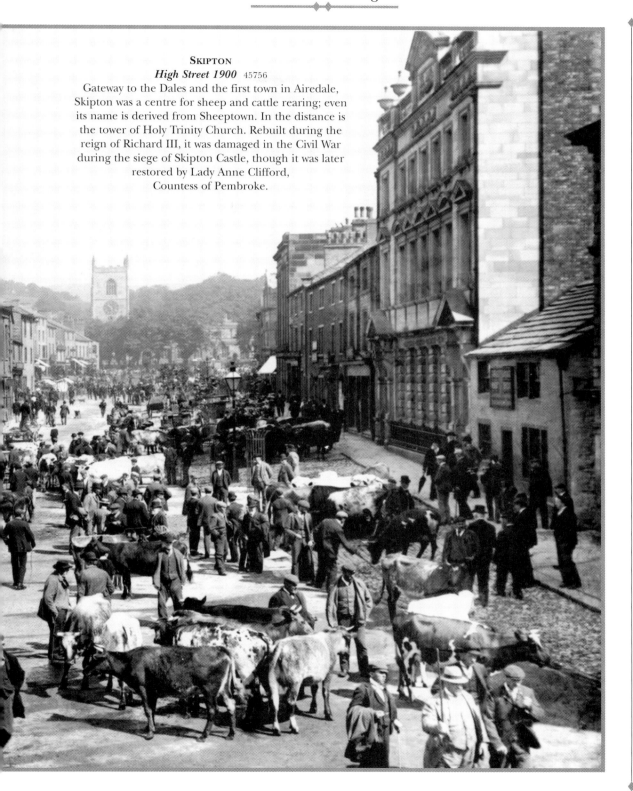

SKIPTON
High Street 1900 45756
Gateway to the Dales and the first town in Airedale,
Skipton was a centre for sheep and cattle rearing; even
its name is derived from Sheeptown. In the distance is
the tower of Holy Trinity Church. Rebuilt during the
reign of Richard III, it was damaged in the Civil War
during the siege of Skipton Castle, though it was later
restored by Lady Anne Clifford,
Countess of Pembroke.

BOLTON ABBEY c1886 18510

This has long been a favourite spot for painters, and was made famous by Landseer. The priory was founded in 1153 by Alicia de Romilly on the site of a Saxon manor. Building continued up to the Dissolution; the west front and west tower were never completed. The nave survived intact to become the parish church.

KILNSEY CRAG 1900 45807

The village below the Crag was once owned by Fountains Abbey, and was the site of a manor court. The Crag itself is probably Wharfedale's most famous landmark. An annual Crag Race to the top and back is held during the Upper Wharfedale Show.

SETTLE, THE TOWN 1903 50134

Across the Ribble from Giggleswick, the small market town of Settle was a good centre for excursions into the surrounding limestone hills. On the right we can see part of the 17th-century shambles with its open-arcaded shops with living accommodation above. On the left is Henson's Temperance Hotel for those who had signed the pledge; for those who hadn't, rooms could be had at the Lion for 3s a night.

SETTLE, DUKE STREET 1903 50136

The town contains a number of substantial houses, one of which is known as The Folly - this is because its builder, Thomas Preston, ran out of money before he could finish it. Though not featured in this picture, the Elizabethan-looking Town Hall was actually completed in 1832.

GIGGLESWICK, THE SCHOOL 1903 50147A

CLAPHAM, THE CHURCH c1881 13673

GIGGLESWICK
The School 1903
Giggleswick School was founded in 1553 and is situated to the west of the village. The large building with the domed roof is the school chapel. When Victoria Cave was discovered in the face of Landcliffe Scar in 1838, it was found to contain bones and tools from the Neolithic period, and relics from its occupation by Romano-British refugees during the mid 5th century. The finds were housed in Giggleswick school-house for many years.

◆

CLAPHAM
The Church c1881
Situated approximately halfway between Settle and Ingleton, Clapham had been a tourist destination since 1857, when Ingleborough Cave was opened to the public. Visitors could get overnight accommodation at either the Flying Horse Shoe or the New Inn.

INGLETON 1890 24157
Ingleton was a small industrial town founded on coal mining, lime burning, and cotton mills. The opening of the railway in the late 1840s turned it into a tourist centre for those wishing to visit nearby waterfalls and caves in the dales of the rivers Twiss and the Doe.

LINTON, THE CHURCH 1900 45787
St Michael's stands on the banks of the River Wharfe about 900 yards northwest of the village. Though mainly built in the 14th century, the church does house a 10th-century brass crucifix.

PATELEY BRIDGE, THE OLD CHURCH 1893 32025
The ruined church of St Mary stands on a hill overlooking Pateley Bridge, a market town since the 14th century and once a centre for lead-mining. Visitors to the churchyard were afforded excellent views of the moors.

RIPON, THE CATHEDRAL c1885 18316
Construction of the present cathedral was begun either by Archbishop Thomas of Bayeux (1070-1100) or Archbishop Thurstan (1114-1134). All that remains of the monastery built by St Wilfred in about 669 is a crypt located under the present cathedral's lantern. Wilfred's building was destroyed by King Eadred in 950, though it is believed it was rebuilt some years later.

RIPON, THE CATHEDRAL LIBRARY c1885 18338

The cathedral library was started in 1624 when Dean Higgin bequeathed his collection of books to the Chapter. Visitors in the 1880s could have inspected a 13th-century illuminated Bible, and an illuminated Psalter once used during festivals associated with St Wilfred.

RIPON, THE CATHEDRAL 1895 35263

The great west front was built in the Early English style between 1215 and 1255. The towers, which are 121 ft high, were once surmounted with spires; the gable end rises 103 ft above street level. The cathedral underwent a major restoration between 1862 and 1870 in the capable hands of Sir George Gilbert Scott.

RIPON

Market Place 1901 47179

Market stalls huddle around the 90 ft obelisk raised in
1781 to commemorate William Aislabie's 60-year stint
in the House of Commons as the local MP. In 1901 the
population of Ripon was about 8200; the weekly
market was held on Thursdays.

FOUNTAINS ABBEY 1886 18352

Visitors to Ripon could hire a carriage to take them on the six-mile round trip to Fountains Abbey, or, if they were feeling up to it, they could walk it. Fountains was founded in poverty in 1132, and building work continued to 1524. At the Dissolution it was sold to Sir Richard Gresham and then to Sir Stephen Proctor, who used some of the stone to build Fountains Hall.

BOROUGHBRIDGE, MARKET PLACE 1895 35287

This is an old market and coaching town on the Great North Road that once supported no less than twenty-two inns. The town dates back to the Norman occupation, when a bridge was built over the River Ure.

BOROUGHBRIDGE, HIGH STREET 1895 35288

To the east of Boroughbridge lies the site of Isurium Brigantium, the capital of the Brigantes and once a supply base for the Ninth Legion. To the west, on the road to Roecliffe, stands the Devil's Arrows. These are standing stones, weighing about 36 tonnes each. It is said that they were originally bolts of lightning fired by the Devil to destroy Boroughbridge.

ALDBOROUGH, THE VILLAGE 1895 35298

The village of Aldborough lies on the site of Isurium Brigantium, and the parish church stands on the site of a Roman temple to Mercury. The cross is said to commemorate the Battle of Boroughbridge, when in 1322 Edward II defeated Thomas, Earl of Lancaster. The Earl sought sanctuary in St Andrew's church, but was dragged off to Pontefract Castle where he was beheaded.

YORK, ST MARY'S ABBEY, EAST END c1880 12945

YORK
St Mary's Abbey, East End c1880

The Benedictine Abbey of St Mary was originally founded in 1089 by William de Lastingham, a nephew of William the Conqueror. Enlarged by William Rufus, the abbey was eventually destroyed by fire; it was rebuilt from 1270 by Simon de Warwick - the reconstruction took twenty-two years. A victim of the Dissolution, the Abbey was used as a quarry, and stone salvaged from it could be found in buildings all over the city.

◆

YORK
The Minster 1893

The Minster towers above Bootham Bar, one of the city's defended gateways, which had retained its barbican until 1832. The Corporation were for pulling them all down, but were stopped in doing so by public outcry.

YORK, THE MINSTER 1893 32032

YORK, THE MINSTER, SOUTH WEST C1880 12894
Begun by Archbishop Walter de Gray during the reign of King John and finally completed in July 1472, York
Minster stands on a site previously occupied by the Roman praetorium and Saxon churches; the earliest of these
was a small wattle oratory constructed for the baptism of Edwin, King of Northumbria, during the Easter
celebrations of 627. The Minster is one of the largest cathedrals in England at over 546 ft in length and 222 ft
across the transepts. The western towers are 196 ft high, whilst the central tower rises over 100 ft above the
intersection of the nave, choir, and transepts.

YORK, LOW PETERGATE 1892 30632
On the right are the Lombard House premises of George Merriman, pawnbroker and jeweller, whose descendants were still trading from the same shop over seventy years later. Note the large brush hanging above Searle's brush and mat warehouse; it is now an exhibit in the Castle Museum.

YORK, THE MERCHANTS' HALL 1893 32040
For three hundred years the Merchant Adventurers of York were the wealthiest and most powerful of the city's guilds. It was built at a time when York was a Staples town for England's principal export, wool. All negotiations, financial arrangements, weighing, and logistics necessary to export a shipment of wool was carried out at the Hall.

YORK

Goodramgate 1892 30631

Here we see Victorian street advertising at its best. Websters are offering to sole and heel men's boots for 2s 6d a pair; women's boots are somewhat cheaper at 1s 6d a pair. John Warton - we believe that is him standing in the doorway - owned The Cheap Shop, an early discount store offering china, glassware, lamps, brushes, wicks, lamp oil and so on at competitive prices. On the right is a small sign advertising W. Ankers, china riveter and repairer.

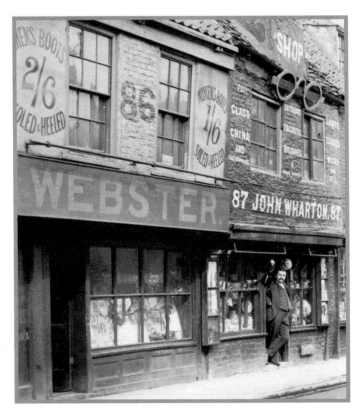

YORK

The Market 1908 59799

A busy market Saturday in Parliament Street. The horse-drawn omnibus has brought in shoppers eager for a bargain or two from one of the outlying villages; good cheese at 6d a pound; 3lb of flour for 5d; a 56lb sack of potatoes for 2s 4d.

YORK
The Station 1909 61850
The magnificent sweep of York station dates from the completion of the Doncaster-Selby-York route. Opened in July 1877, the station allowed through running of trains. The old station it replaced lay just within the city walls; its site and layout were such that trains had either to back in or out of it.

YORK, THE SHAMBLES 1893 32043

Between King's Square and Pavement, the Shambles were once known as the Fleshammels, or butchers' street, and in this picture several of the late 13th- to early 14th-century shops were still fulfilling that role.

YORK
The River Ouse c1885

A Humber keel boat discharges cargo at York. Despite its cumbersome looks, this keel boat could carry about fifty tonnes and was extremely manoeuvrable; it was capable of sailing close to the wind, and it could be handled by one man. Their origins are obscure, but their rig suggests that they might be a direct descendant of the Viking trading vessels that once plied the Humber, Ouse, Trent, Don and Derwent.

YORK
The Cavalry Barracks 1886

Imphal Barracks covered a huge area, and could house at least one cavalry regiment and an infantry battalion, as well as providing support for reservists, volunteer units and recruit training. In 1886 the resident cavalry regiment was the 3rd Hussars, some of whom are seen here at sabre practice.

YORK, THE RIVER OUSE C1885 18455

YORK, THE CAVALRY BARRACKS 1886 18717

Filey Brigg 1890 23489

At low tide the mile-long reef of rock known as Filey Brigg was a favourite spot for Victorian holidaymakers, amateur geologists, and fossil-hunters alike. Here they could explore ledges around the cliff, caves, caverns and pools. The Brigg forms a natural breakwater for Filey which lies to the south.

Filey, The Spa 1890 23477

Eight miles south of Scarborough, Filey was a fishing port, and its parish church once belonged to Bridlington Priory. One of Filey's hotels, The Crescent, was quite expensive in 1906 at 5s 6d for a room and 5s for dinner. Foord's and the Three Tuns, however, offered an all-in daily rate of 6s 6d per person.

FILEY
The Promenade 1901
For many years it was a working fishing port, but Filey's popularity as a holiday destination took off in the 1890s. It was a place for those seeking a quiet holiday away from the more developed resorts such as Bridlington and Scarborough.

FILEY
The Sands 1897
Visitors had a choice between a donkey ride or a trip along the sands in small horse-drawn carriages, one of which can seen in the background. Just coming into view on the right is one of Archibald Ramsden's bathing machines for those wishing to avail themselves of a more discreet way of taking a plunge in the bay.

FILEY, THE PROMENADE 1901 48019

FILEY, THE SANDS 1897 39344

BRIDLINGTON, PRINCESS STREET 1897 39371
Bridlington was within easy reach of trippers from Yorkshire's industrial heartland; its population of 13,000 more than doubled during the holiday period. During the summer season, a coach plied between Bridlington and Scarborough via Filey; fares were 8s return, 5s one way, and to Filey 3s single, 5s return.

BRIDLINGTON, PRINCE'S PARADE 1906 55752
A well laid out promenade was guaranteed to bring the trippers into town. Bridlington was renowned for its flower beds and litter-free walks.

HULL, MARKET PLACE 1903 49809

By the beginning of the 20th century, Hull had a population in excess of 238,000; it was the third largest port in Britain, with docks running for several miles along the north bank of the Humber. In 1903 its deep-sea fishing fleet, which numbered several hundred vessels, landed a combined catch of over 79,000 tonnes.

HULL 1903 49816

Electric trams were introduced on 5 July 1899; stopping places were indicated by white poles on the pavement edge. The trams ran to various suburbs, and routes originated from either Victoria Square, Savile Street or King Edward Street. During 1898-99 the tramway took delivery of 24 double-deck trailers, the idea being that these could be towed behind trams during busy periods. The trailers only survived for a few months before the decision was taken to motorise them.

BEVERLEY, MARKET PLACE 1894 34795

The county town of the East Riding, Beverley grew up around a monastery founded in Saxon times. The town was incorporated in 1129 by Archbishop Thurstan of York, and as well as its minster it has another fine church in the shape of St Mary's. Originally a chapel to the minster, St Mary's is noted for its Decorated chancel, Perpendicular nave and a central tower dating from the 16th century. This tower was erected in place of an earlier one which collapsed in 1520, badly damaging the north aisle arcade. In the picture is the rather pleasant market cross of 1714.

BEVERLEY, THE MINSTER 1894 34778

Beverley Minster was begun in 1220, with construction starting at what is now the east end. The magnificent west end, which resembles York Minster, was completed in 1420. Overall the Minster is 334 ft long and 64 ft wide, and the west towers stand 200 ft high. Inside there is the fridstol, or chair of peace, a relic of the time when Beverley enjoyed the privilege of inviolable sanctuary. Any fugitive who reached the chair could claim the protection of the Church from the law.

BEDALE, MARKET PLACE 1908 59516

The sloping cobbled market place appears to be the venue for a fair; we can make out a showman's engine and a caravan, and what might be a stall. The church is dedicated to St Gregory. Its 14th- and 15th-century tower features a first-floor room protected by a portcullis. The tower might have served as a defensive position during Scottish raids.

BEDALE, THE VILLAGE 1896 38283

This photograph was taken from the tower of St Gregory's. We can see the wide part of the main street that served as the market place; in 1896 there was plenty of room for retailers to spread their wares out into the street.

SNAPE CASTLE 1900 45620

To the northeast of Masham and three miles south of Bedale, Snape Castle was once the home of Catherine Parr, sixth and last wife of Henry VIII. Dating from the 15th and 16th century, Snape was once a stronghold of the Neville family.

MASHAM, MARKET PLACE 1908 60697

Masham received its market charter in 1250 and became known for its sheep fairs; you can see the pens in the background. The market would bring in farmers and dealers from miles around; with up to 80,000 sheep and lambs being offered for sale.

MASHAM
Market Place 1908

Here we have a closer look at the tower of St Mary's Church. The lower part is Norman, and the octagonal lantern and spire were added in the 15th century. The church was wealthy, almost certainly benefiting from the sheep fairs, and was said to be the richest prebend in Yorkshire, if not the whole of England.

◆

EAST WITTON
The Village 1896

East Witton lies between Jervaulx Abbey and Middleham. Somewhere in the woods on nearby Witton Fell is a spring with a grotto. The grotto was built as a folly by the Marquess of Ailesbury in 1817 and is known locally as either Tilsey Folly or Slobbering Sal.

MASHAM, MARKET PLACE 1908 60699

EAST WITTON, THE VILLAGE 1896 38265

MIDDLEHAM, THE CASTLE AND CROSS 1896 38272

Construction of Middleham Castle began in about 1170; work carried on through the 13th and 14th centuries. The northeast tower was modified in the 14th century into a three-storey gatehouse with a drawbridge and portcullis. Middleham eventually passed by marriage into the hands of the powerful Neville family, though in 1471 it was given to Richard, Duke of Gloucester at his marriage. After Bosworth it was owned by Henry VII.

MIDDLEHAM, MARKET PLACE AND THE CROSS 1908 59537

Middleham was the former capital of Wensleydale and a market town. As well as the weekly market there were annual fairs, and the close proximity of two abbeys must also have stimulated trade. Four miles southwest stood the great Cistercian abbey of Jervaulx, and two miles to the southwest was the Praemonstratensian abbey of Coverham.

MIDDLEHAM, THE CHURCH 1902 48947
The parish church, dedicated to St Alkelda and St Mary, dates from the 14th century, and was raised to collegiate status by Richard, Duke of Gloucester. The tradition is that Alkelda was a Saxon lady strangled near the town by some Danish women.

LEYBURN, FROM THE TOWN HALL 1896 38252
We are looking towards the shambles and the parish church. Though Leyburn was a market town, it did not have its own church until 1836. The shambles were demolished in 1931.

LEYBURN
Market Place 1889 21690
In the 1890s the market rights were still owned by
Lord Bolton, the charter having been granted by
Charles I. Originally markets were held on a Tuesday,
but this was changed to Fridays in 1696.

WENSLEY, THE GREEN AND THE CHURCH 1893 33137

Wensley in the 1890s was a small village, but back in the 14th century it was a thriving market town. In 1563 Wensleydale was devastated by plague; those who could manage to do so appear to have fled Wensley, and the dead were buried in plague pits in a field known as Chapel Hill.

WENSLEY, THE GREEN AND POST OFFICE 1893 33138

Holy Trinity dates mainly from the 13th and 14th centuries, though it is thought to stand on the site of an earlier Saxon church. The church contains an old box which might be the reliquary from Easby Abbey that once housed St Agatha's bones. The old elm tree on the green is said to have been planted in 1690, and was used for shade by John Wesley when he preached here. It was blown down by gale-force winds in 1946.

REDMIRE
The Village 1896
The agricultural village of Redmire, near Bolton Castle, was once a centre for coal and lead-mining.

◆

WEST BURTON
The Village 1889
It looks for all the world as though someone has chopped the spire off a church and deposited it in the middle of the village. This is, however, the village cross. It was erected in 1820 and restored in the late 1880s.

REDMIRE, THE VILLAGE 1896 38263

WEST BURTON, THE VILLAGE 1889 21676

WEST BURTON, THE VILLAGE 1909 61757

Here we see an almost deserted village. There was a time when it was company policy at Frith to take pictures with as few people as possible on them. This was purely for commercial reasons: Frith wanted to keep postcards in publication for as long as possible, and wanted nothing on them which might date them, such as fashions. West Burton was once a busy industrial hamlet of hand knitters, dyers and wool combers.

AYSGARTH, THE VILLAGE 1908 60788

Victorian visitors to Aysgarth came to look at the large parish church dedicated to St Andrew, and to see the falls, a series of cascades extending for half a mile on the River Ure. The best view of the Upper Falls was from a 16th-century bridge over the river.

CARPERBY, THE VILLAGE 1909 61764
The cross, erected in 1674, marks the centre of this agricultural community with strong Quaker connections; the meeting house was one of the largest buildings in the village.

NAPPA HALL 1889 21665
Nappa Hall stands between Carperby and Askrigg, and was once the seat of the Metcalfe family; Sir Christopher Metcalfe was acting Sheriff of Yorkshire in the early 17th century. James I stayed at Nappa Hall when hunting in the Forest of Wensleydale. The Metcalfes were once the master foresters.

ASKRIGG, THE VILLAGE 1906 56017

Askrigg was already prosperous when the Domesday Book was being compiled. It remained the leading industrial and commercial centre for Upper Wensleydale until 1699, when Hawes was granted its charter. Even in the 12th century Askrigg had a large church, though it was replaced in the 1240s. The tower was added in the 15th century.

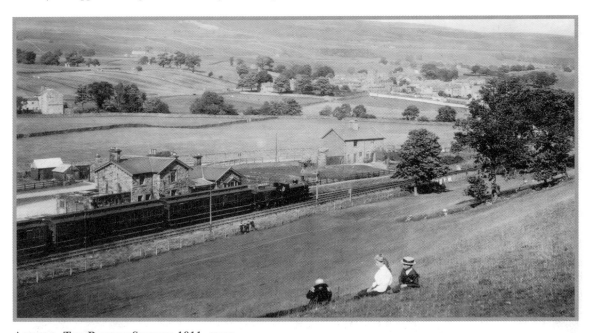

ASKRIGG, THE RAILWAY STATION 1911 63466

Askrigg station is on the North Eastern Railway route between Northallerton and a connection with the Midland Railway at Hawes. Askrigg closed to passengers in April 1954, but remained open for goods traffic for another ten years.

BAINBRIDGE
The Village 1889
Bainbridge stands astride the River Bane, which at just three miles in length is said to be the shortest river in England. It flows from Semerwater, which with a surface area of about ninety acres was the largest lake in the North Riding, to the River Ure.

BAINBRIDGE
The Green 1906
Though the village stands on England's smallest river, it probably had one of the largest greens. Bainbridge was once an important crossroads where roads from Lancaster, Swaledale, and Westmoreland met; it was also a settlement for woodsmen working in the great forest of Wensleydale.

BAINBRIDGE, THE VILLAGE 1889 21661

BAINBRIDGE, THE GREEN 1906 56024

HAWES, THE SCHOOL AND VILLAGE 1900 45635

Hawes is not mentioned in the Domesday Book; it appears that a settlement of sorts was established here in about 1227. The village grew slowly until 1699, when it was granted a market charter by William III. It later became a centre for textiles, quarrying and the production of Wensleydale cheese. Cheese production had been farmhouse-based, but towards the end of the 19th century a factory was built just off the Gayle road. The original cheese as made by the monks of Jervaulx used ewes' milk; later, farmhouse and factory cheese was made from milk from shorthorn cows.

HAWES, TOWN FOOT 1900 45634

St Margaret's Church was originally built during the reign of Richard III, but it was replaced in 1851 with the structure shown here. A travel guide for 1900 states that Hawes 'is a good centre for excursions to Hardraw Force, via the Buttertubs Pass to Muker, in Swaledale, etc - at Hawes Junction we join the Midland Railway'.

HARDRAW, THE VILLAGE 1900 45646

Hardraw lies just to the north of Hawes; it is noted for Hardraw Force, a 98 ft high waterfall, which in times of severe weather conditions freezes over. It had happened in a spectacular way in 1881, so there would have people on hand to tell our cameramen all about it. Visitors to Hardraw Force can walk on a path behind the fall.

RICHMOND, THE CASTLE AND THE BRIDGE 1892 30654

The Norman fortress at Richmond commands the entrance to Swaledale. Construction began in 1072, though the massive keep dates from the 12th century. The building at the far right of the castle is Scollard's Hall, built 1080 and thought to be the oldest domestic building in England.

RICHMOND
Market Place 1908 59492
Market day at Richmond. The first recorded market took place here in 1155; by 1440 the town was trading in variety of commodities, ranging from dairy produce, wine and fish, to coal, lead-ore, copper and silk. Holy Trinity is an unusual building in that several shops, such as the one occupied by King & Son, were built onto it.

EASBY ABBEY 1898 41655

The abbey was founded by Roald, Constable of Richmond Castle in 1155, for the Praemonstratensian Order, or White Canons as they were sometimes called. The remains include the refectory, the infirmary, and parts of the abbey church.

GUISBOROUGH, HIGH STREET 1891 29210

Guisborough was the ancient capital of Cleveland, and once the location of an abbey founded by Robert de Brus. In May 1822 a spring was discovered about one mile to the south-west, and Guisborough climbed aboard the spa town bandwagon. The spring was said to relieve rheumatism and bilious complaints, and was an excellent diuretic.

GUISBOROUGH, MARKET PLACE 1899 44756

Walter Wilson, on the left, the largest grocers in town, was offering rich, strong Indian tea at 1s 8d a pound, as well as regular savings on bacon, hams, cheese and lard. Next to Wilson's is the bay-windowed Buck Hotel; note the buck over the entrance. Across the street is Fairburn's the druggists, and facing us is Jackson's boot and shoe shop.

MIDDLESBROUGH, THE MARKET PLACE 1913 66408.

On the left is the old Town Hall, built in the mid 1840s when the town's population was about 6000 and growing fast. It was replaced in 1889 by a much larger one, designed by Alfred Waterhouse and costing £130,000.

MIDDLESBROUGH, CORPORATION ROAD 1901 47979

The electric street tramway system operated on 3ft 6in gauge track and opened in 1898. Once the infrastructure was in place, the operational cost of electric trams was about 6d per mile, whereas horse-drawn trams cost about 9d per mile.

MIDDLESBROUGH, ALBERT PARK GATES 1896 37574

Opened in 1868 by Prince Arthur, Duke of Connaught, Albert Park was developed upon land purchased for the town by Henry Bolckow. It provided workers with somewhere close at hand to go to escape the grime and the grit of foundry, shipyard, and engineering works.

REDCAR, FROM THE PIER 1896 37593

Redcar was to Middlesbrough what Tynemouth and Whitley Bay were to Newcastle: a handy resort less than one hour's travel away by train. However, Redcar, and all other seaside resorts served by the North Eastern Railway, suffered for years because of the reluctance of the railway to run Sunday services in case it upset churchgoers.

REDCAR, HIGH STREET 1906 54451A

Horse-drawn cabs ply the High Street, and retailers spread their wares out onto the pavement in the anticipation of attracting a few sales. One guide-book for the period described the resort as 'frequented by the workpeople of Middlesbrough, Darlington &c. The great attraction of Redcar lies in its almost unlimited sands'.

REDCAR

The Pier 1896 37594

Redcar's expanse of superb sands on three beaches, one of which is nearly a mile wide at low water, was ideal for those needing to take a constitutional. In the 1860s a local doctor wrote that 'Redcar is adapted to the debilitated class of invalids not only by reason of its powerful tonic atmosphere and excellent bathing but because of the natural facilities offered by its extensive beach for easy exercise and locomotion'.

MARSKE-BY-THE-SEA
Fuland Terrace 1906
Situated in the centre of the bay
between Redcar and Saltburn, Marske in
Victorian and Edwardian times was the
smaller of the three resorts and
lacked amenities.

MARSKE-BY-THE-SEA
The Old Church c1885
The old church of St Germain is
perched on the cliff top. All that remains
today is the steepled tower.

MARSKE-BY-THE-SEA, FULAND TERRACE 1906 54844

MARSKE-BY-THE-SEA, THE OLD CHURCH c1885 18128

SALTBURN-BY-THE-SEA 1891 29195
Rugged cliffs facing the sea and the moors inland were what brought Victorian and Edwardian visitors to Saltburn. On the right is part of the original village.

SALTBURN-BY-THE-SEA 1885 18104
This picture shows us some of the late Victorian development at Saltburn: large hotels and villas are built on a cliff away from the old village, part of which is in the foreground.

SKELTON CASTLE 1891
Situated three miles north of
Guisborough, Skelton Castle is a
battlemented country house dating from
about 1800. There was a castle here in
the 12th century, and at one time it was
owned by the de Brus family.

◆

STAITHES
Baiting the Lines c1900
Staithes was a fishing port of some
standing, landing sufficient cod,
mackerel and haddock for the North
Eastern Railway to run three or four
special fish trains a week. Lining was one
method by which the fish were caught.

SKELTON CASTLE 1891 29206

STAITHES, BAITING THE LINES c1900 S176001

RUNSWICK FROM THE BEACH C1885 18199
Rugged cliffs provide the backdrop to Runswick; houses were perched wherever it seemed most suitable at the time to build them.

RUNSWICK, FROM THE BEACH C1885 18198
Even when not fishing, there was always maintenance work to be done on the boats, or nets to mend and lines to bait.

SANDSEND 1901 46809

Sandsend is just three miles north of Whitby. Two becks twist and turn through the village on their way to the sea, and, as we can see here, many of the cottages cling to the sides of the ravines. At one time many villagers found employment in the local alum works, but this has long since closed down.

RUSWARP, THE BRIDGE C1881 14491

Ruswarp is situated on the banks of the Esk just inland from Whitby, and there was once a mill here that belonged to the Abbey. Fifty years or so after this picture was taken the bridge was badly damaged during severe flooding. The Whitby lifeboat came up the river to rescue people marooned by the water.

WHITBY, EAST CLIFF 1901 46779

WHITBY
East Cliff 1901

We are looking towards the East Cliff, where the old parish church of St Mary's and the ruins of Whitby Abbey stand. St Mary's is 12th-century, consisting of a nave, chancel, and tower. Though the exterior is plain, the interior is one of the most outstanding in England. There are galleries on every side; box pews dating back to the 17th century; a three-decker pulpit of 1778; and all is lit by candlelight. The church was made famous by Bram Stoker in his Gothic novel 'Dracula' as the place where the count sought refuge in the grave of a suicide.

WHITBY
A Fisher Girl 1891

For centuries the people of Whitby earned their living from the sea; some still do. The town was once a whaling port, and there were blubber houses along the inner harbour. Between 1766 and 1816 the local whaling fleet caught 2761 whales and about 25,000 seals.

WHITBY, A FISHER GIRL 1891 28868

WHITBY
St Hilda's Abbey 1891

It was here in 657 that a monastery was founded by St Hilda for the Christian King Oswy of Northumbria in thanks to God for his victory over the Mercians and their pagan King Penda. Open to both men and women, Whitby became one of the most influential monasteries in the Celtic world. It was noted for its learning, and turned out a number of 7th-century scholars, including Bosa, Oftor and John, as well as Caedmon, the acknowledged father of the sacred song. After being destroyed by the Danes in 867, Whitby was not refounded until 1078, when the Benedictines began building their Abbey.

WHITBY
From Lar Pool c1881

At this date Whitby had a shipbuilding industry. In 1840 Thomas Turnbull opened the Whitehall Dockyard, which is at centre right in the picture. In 1871 Turnbulls switched to building iron tramps, and 113 were built between then and the yard's closure in 1902. Of the total, 60 tramps were built for the Turnbull family themselves; they operated fleets out of Whitby, Cardiff and London. The reason for the yard's closure was that Whitby bridge restricted dimensions to a maximum beam of 44 ft.

WHITBY, ST HILDA'S ABBEY 1891   28859

WHITBY, FROM LAR POOL c1881   14465

ROBIN HOOD'S BAY 1886 18195
Robin Hood's Bay was a fishing community six miles south of Whitby, though a number of sail colliers and coastal trading vessels worked from here. It was also home to some serious smuggling; by 1800 the revenue believed that every household was involved in the honest trade in one way or another.

ROBIN HOOD'S BAY c1885 18193
Fishermen stand on the slope that leads from the sea into the village. Behind them is the lifeboat station, and to the right, protected by a sea wall, is the Bay Hotel, or rather the second Bay Hotel. The first was a little nearer to the sea, and collapsed into it in 1834.

RAVENSCAR 1901 46802

Ravenscar stands on a plateau 600 ft above sea level at the southern end of Robin Hood's Bay. There were once plans to turn it into a resort to rival Scarborough, but the scheme failed owing to the unstable geology of the area. The Romans had a signal station here in 400; a stone inscription was unearthed during the building of Ravenshill Hall in the 1770s.

SCARBOROUGH, NORTH BAY 1897 39463

A band concert attracts a sizeable crowd in Clarence Gardens. Approaching our cameraman are two soldiers dressed in their walking-out uniforms. It is unusual at this period to find pictures of soldiers walking out in public with an arm around a lady; such conduct was forbidden under queen's regulations. On the other hand, sailors belonging to the Royal Navy were under no such restrictions.

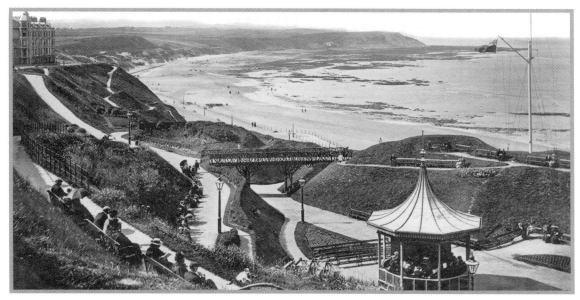

SCARBOROUGH, NORTH BAY 1897 39465

It was the construction of the Marine Drive around the base of Castle Hill that spurred on the development of the North Bay and the northern part of the town. This view looks towards Northstead Manor, which, like the Chiltern Hundreds, provides an appointment of steward and bailiff for members of the House of Commons who wish to resign their seats.

SCARBOROUGH, CASTLE HILL 1890 23469

Castle Hill is a promontory which rises nearly 300 ft above sea level and separates the north and south bays. The fortress, which dates back to the 12th century, was twice besieged during the English Civil War, and on both occasions the garrison surrendered to the Parliamentarians. During the late 19th century, it was still being used by volunteer artillery units for gun drills and firing practice.

SCARBOROUGH 1897 39460
The imposing bulk of the 300-bed Grand Hotel
dominates this picture of the South Bay. At this time
Scarborough was by far the most popular east coast
resort in the north of England; it was noted for its
bracing air and beaches ideal for bathing.

SCARBOROUGH 1891 28810

Boatmen stand at the waters' edge attempting to persuade visitors to take an excursion round the bay. In the centre of the picture a small group of intending passengers waits to clamber aboard a cart, which will then be pushed out to a boat. Further across the picture you can see a wheeled landing stage in use.

SCARBOROUGH, CHILDREN'S CORNER 1890 23454

Alas, we have no idea what is going on in the foreground, but it certainly involves the children. It could be anything from some sort of entertainment to a works, church, or chapel outing. In the background is the Spa Promenade, one of the town's main attractions in the 1890s. The South Cliff Tramway offered an alternative means of escape from the beach to the Esplanade; the other way was by 224 steps cutting through the Spa Gardens.

Index

Frith Book Co Titles

Frith Book Company publish over 100 new titles each year. For latest catalogue please contact Frith Book Co.

Town Books 96pp, 100 photos. County and Themed Books 128pp, 150 photos
(unless specified) All titles hardback laminated case and jacket
except those indicated pb (paperback)

Around Bakewell	1-85937-113-2	£12.99	Isle of Man	1-85937-065-9	£14.99
Around Barnstaple	1-85937-084-5	£12.99	Isle of Wight	1-85937-114-0	£14.99
Around Bath	1-85937-097-7	£12.99	Around Leicester	1-85937-073-x	£12.99
Around Blackpool	1-85937-049-7	£12.99	Around Lincoln	1-85937-111-6	£12.99
Around Bognor Regis	1-85937-055-1	£12.99	Around Liverpool	1-85937-051-9	£12.99
Around Bournemouth	1-85937-067-5	£12.99	Around Maidstone	1-85937-056-X	£12.99
Around Bristol	1-85937-050-0	£12.99	North Yorkshire	1-85937-048-9	£14.99
British Life A Century Ago	1-85937-103-5	£17.99	Northumberland and Tyne & Wear		
Around Cambridge	1-85937-092-6	£12.99		1-85937-072-1	£14.99
Cambridgeshire	1-85937-086-1	£14.99	Around Nottingham	1-85937-060-8	£12.99
Cheshire	1-85937-045-4	£14.99	Around Oxford	1-85937-096-9	£12.99
Around Chester	1-85937-090-X	£12.99	Oxfordshire	1-85937-076-4	£14.99
Around Chesterfield	1-85937-071-3	£12.99	Around Penzance	1-85937-069-1	£12.99
Around Chichester	1-85937-089-6	£12.99	Around Plymouth	1-85937-119-1	£12.99
Cornwall	1-85937-054-3	£14.99	Around Reading	1-85937-087-X	£12.99
Cotswolds	1-85937-099-3	£14.99	Around St Ives	1-85937-068-3	£12.99
Cumbria	1-85937-101-9	£14.99	Around Salisbury	1-85937-091-8	£12.99
Around Derby	1-85937-046-2	£12.99	Around Scarborough	1-85937-104-3	£12.99
Devon	1-85937-052-7	£14.99	Scottish Castles	1-85937-077-2	£14.99
Dorset	1-85937-075-6	£14.99	Around Sevenoaks and Tonbridge		
Dorset Coast	1-85937-062-4	£14.99		1-85937-057-8	£12.99
Down the Thames	1-85937-121-3	£14.99	Sheffield and S Yorkshire	1-85937-070-5	£14.99
Around Dublin	1-85937-058-6	£12.99	Around Southport	1-85937-106-x	£12.99
East Anglia	1-85937-059-4	£14.99	Around Shrewsbury	1-85937-110-8	£12.99
Around Eastbourne	1-85937-061-6	£12.99	Shropshire	1-85937-083-7	£14.99
English Castles	1-85937-078-0	£14.99	South Devon Coast	1-85937-107-8	£14.99
Essex	1-85937-082-9	£14.99	Staffordshire (96pp)	1-85937-047-0	£12.99
Around Exeter	1-85937-126-4	£12.99	Around Stratford upon Avon		
Around Falmouth	1-85937-066-7	£12.99		1-85937-098-5	£12.99
Around Great Yarmouth	1-85937-085-3	£12.99	Suffolk	1-85937-074-8	£14.99
Greater Manchester	1-85937-108-6	£14.99	Surrey	1-85937-081-0	£14.99
Hampshire	1-85937-064-0	£14.99	Around Torbay	1-85937-063-2	£12.99
Around Harrogate	1-85937-112-4	£12.99	Welsh Castles	1-85937-120-5	£14.99
Hertfordshire	1-85937-079-9	£14.99	West Midlands	1-85937-109-4	£14.99
			Wiltshire	1-85937-053-5	£14.99

Frith Book Co Titles Available in 2000

Canals and Waterways	1-85937-129-9	£17.99	Apr
Around Guildford	1-85937-117-5	£12.99	Apr
Around Horsham	1-85937-127-2	£12.99	Apr
Around Ipswich	1-85937-133-7	£12.99	Apr
Ireland (pb)	1-85937-181-7	£9.99	Apr
London (pb)	1-85937-183-3	£9.99	Apr
New Forest	1-85937-128-0	£14.99	Apr
Around Newark	1-85937-105-1	£12.99	Apr
Around Newquay	1-85937-140-x	£12.99	Apr
Scotland (pb)	1-85937-182-5	£9.99	Apr
Around Southampton	1-85937-088-8	£12.99	Apr
Sussex (pb)	1-85937-184-1	£9.99	Apr
Around Winchester	1-85937-139-6	£12.99	Apr
Around Belfast	1-85937-094-2	£12.99	May
Colchester (pb)	1-85937-188-4	£8.99	May
Dartmoor	1-85937-145-0	£14.99	May
Exmoor	1-85937-132-9	£14.99	May
Leicestershire (pb)	1-85937-185-x	£9.99	May
Lincolnshire	1-85937-135-3	£14.99	May
North Devon Coast	1-85937-146-9	£14.99	May
Nottinghamshire (pb)	1-85937-187-6	£9.99	May
Peak District	1-85937-100-0	£14.99	May
Redhill to Reigate	1-85937-137-x	£12.99	May
Around Truro	1-85937-147-7	£12.99	May
Yorkshire (pb)	1-85937-186-8	£9.99	May
Berkshire (pb)	1-85937-191-4	£9.99	Jun
Brighton (pb)	1-85937-192-2	£8.99	Jun
Churches of Berkshire	1-85937-170-1	£17.99	Jun
Churches of Dorset	1-85937-172-8	£17.99	Jun
Derbyshire (pb)	1-85937-196-5	£9.99	Jun
East Sussex	1-85937-130-2	£14.99	Jun
Edinburgh (pb)	1-85937-193-0	£8.99	Jun
Norwich (pb)	1-85937-194-9	£8.99	Jun
South Devon Living Memories			
	1-85937-168-x	£14.99	Jun

Stone Circles & Ancient Monuments			
	1-85937-143-4	£17.99	Jun
Victorian & Edwardian Kent			
	1-85937-149-3	£14.99	Jun
Warwickshire (pb)	1-85937-203-1	£9.99	Jun
Buckinghamshire (pb)	1-85937-200-7	£9.99	Jul
Down the Severn	1-85937-118-3	£14.99	Jul
Kent (pb)	1-85937-189-2	£9.99	Jul
Victorian & Edwardian Yorkshire			
	1-85937-154-x	£14.99	Jul
West Sussex	1-85937-148-5	£14.99	Jul
Cornish Coast	1-85937-163-9	£14.99	Aug
County Durham	1-85937-123-x	£14.99	Aug
Croydon Living Memories	1-85937-162-0	£12.99	Aug
Dorsert Living Memories	1-85937-210-4	£14.99	Aug
Glasgow (pb)	1-85937-190-6	£8.99	Aug
Gloucestershire	1-85937-102-7	£14.99	Aug
Herefordshire	1-85937-174-4	£14.99	Aug
Kent Living Memories	1-85937-125-6	£14.99	Aug
Lancashire (pb)	1-85937-197-3	£9.99	Aug
Manchester (pb)	1-85937-198-1	£8.99	Aug
North London	1-85937-206-6	£14.99	Aug
Somerset	1-85937-153-1	£14.99	Aug
Tees Valley & Cleveland	1-85937-211-2	£14.99	Aug
Worcestershire	1-85937-152-3	£14.99	Aug
Victorian & Edwardian Maritime Album			
	1-85937-144-2	£17.99	Aug

Available from your local bookshop or from the publisher

FRITH PRODUCTS & SERVICES

Francis Frith would doubtless be pleased to know that the pioneering publishing venture he started in 1860 still continues today. More than a hundred and thirty years later, The Francis Frith Collection continues in the same innovative tradition and is now one of the foremost publishers of vintage photographs in the world. Some of the current activities include:

Interior Decoration

Today Frith's photographs can be seen framed and as giant wall murals in thousands of pubs, restaurants, hotels, banks, retail stores and other public buildings throughout the country. In every case they enhance the unique local atmosphere of the places they depict and provide reminders of gentler days in an increasingly busy and frenetic world.

Product Promotions

Frith products have been used by many major companies to promote the sales of their own products or to reinforce their own history and heritage. Brands include Hovis bread, Courage beers, Scots Porage Oats, Colman's mustard, Cadbury's foods, Mellow Birds coffee, Dunhill pipe tobacco, Guinness, and Bulmer's Cider.

Genealogy and Family History

As the interest in family history and roots grows world-wide, more and more people are turning to Frith's photographs of Great Britain for images of the towns, villages and streets where their ancestors lived; and, of course, photographs of the churches and chapels where their ancestors were christened, married and buried are an essential part of every genealogy tree and family album.

A series of easy-to-use CD Roms is planned for publication, and an increasing number of Frith photographs will be able to be viewed on specialist genealogy sites. A growing range of Frith books will be available on CD.

Frith Products

All Frith photographs are available Framed or just as Mounted Prints, and can be ordered from the address below. From time to time other products - Address Books, Calendars, Table Mats, etc - are available.

The Internet

Already thousands of Frith photographs can be viewed and purchased on the internet. By the end of the year 2000 some 60,000 Frith photographs will be available on the internet. The number of sites is constantly expanding, each focussing on different products and services from the Collection.

Some of the sites are listed below.

www.townpages.co.uk

www.icollector.com

www.barclaysquare.co.uk

www.cornwall-online.co.uk

For more detailed information on Frith companies and products, look at these sites:

www.francisfrith.co.uk

www.frithbook.co.uk

www.francisfrith.com

See the complete list of Frith Books at:

www.frithbook.co.uk

This web site is regularly updated with the latest list of publications from the Frith Book Company Ltd. If you wish to buy books relating to another part of the country that your local bookshop does not stock, you may purchase on-line.

For further information, trade, or author enquiries please contact us at the address below:
The Francis Frith Collection, Frith's Barn, Teffont, Salisbury, Wiltshire, England SP3 5QP.
Tel: +44 (0)1722 716 376 Fax: +44 (0)1722 716 881 Email: uksales@francisfrith.com

To receive your FREE Mounted Print

Mounted Print
Overall size 14 x 11 inches

Cut out this Voucher and return it with your remittance for £1.50 to cover postage and handling.
Choose any photograph included in this book. Your SEPIA print will be A4 in size, and mounted in a cream mount with burgundy rule lines, overall size 14 x 11 inches.

Order additional Mounted Prints at HALF PRICE (only £7.49 each*)

If there are further pictures you would like to order, possibly as gifts for friends and family, acquire them at half price (no additional postage and handling required).

Have your Mounted Prints framed*

For an additional £14.95 per print you can have your chosen Mounted Print framed in an elegant polished wood and gilt moulding, overall size 16 x 13 inches (no additional postage and handling required).

> *** IMPORTANT!**
> These special prices are only available if ordered using the original voucher on this page (no copies permitted) and at the same time as your free Mounted Print, for delivery to the same address

Frith Collectors' Guild

From time to time we publish a magazine of news and stories about Frith photographs and further special offers of Frith products. If you would like 12 months FREE membership, please return this form.

Send completed forms to:
The Francis Frith Collection, Frith's Barn, Teffont, Salisbury, Wiltshire SP3 5QP

Voucher for FREE and Reduced Price Frith Prints

Picture no.	Page number	Qty	Mounted @ £7.49	Framed + £14.95	Total Cost
		1	**Free of charge***	£	£
			£7.49	£	£
			£7.49	£	£
			£7.49	£	£
			£7.49	£	£
			£7.49	£	£

Please allow 28 days for delivery	* Post & handling	£1.50
Book Title	**Total Order Cost**	£

Please do not photocopy this voucher. Only the original is valid, so please cut it out and return it to us.

I enclose a cheque / postal order for £ . . . .
made payable to 'The Francis Frith Collection'
OR please debit my Mastercard / Visa / Switch / Amex card

Number . . . .

Expires . . . . Signature . . . .

Name Mr/Mrs/Ms . . . .

Address . . . .

. . . .

. . . .

. . . . Postcode . . . .

Daytime Tel No . . . .   Valid to 31/12/01

The Francis Frith Collectors' Guild

Please enrol me as a member for 12 months free of charge.

Name Mr/Mrs/Ms . . . .

Address . . . .

. . . .

. . . .

. . . . Postcode . . . .

Free Print - see overleaf